tourism TATTLER

Issue 05 (May) 2015

PUBLISHER
Tourism Tattler (Pty) Ltd.
PO Box 891, Umhlanga Rocks, 4320
KwaZulu-Natal, South Africa.
Website: www.tourismtattler.com

EXECUTIVE EDITOR Des Langkilde
Cell: +27 (0)82 374 7260
Fax: +27 (0)86 651 8080
E-mail: editor@tourismtattler.com
Skype: tourismtattler

MAGAZINE ADVERTISING
ADVERTISING DIRECTOR Bev Langkilde
Cell: +27 (0)71 224 9971
Fax: +27 (0)86 656 3860
E-mail: bev@tourismtattler.com
Skype: bevtourismtattler

SUBSCRIPTIONS
www.tourismtattler.com/subscribe

GREEN KEEP IT ON SCREEN

BACK ISSUES (Click on the covers below).

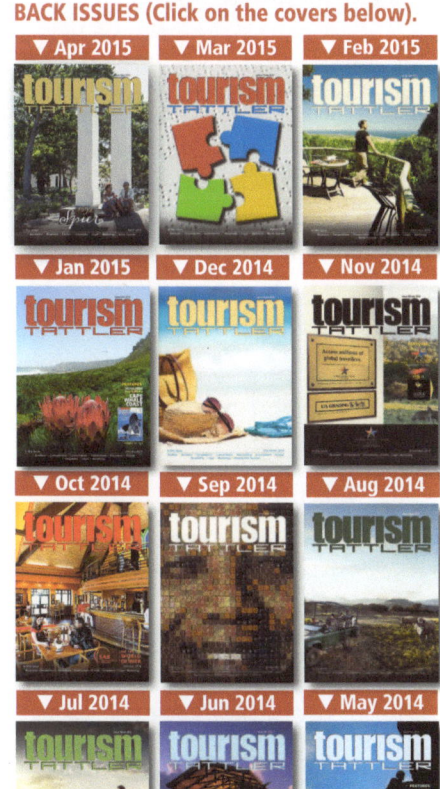

▼ Apr 2015 ▼ Mar 2015 ▼ Feb 2015
▼ Jan 2015 ▼ Dec 2014 ▼ Nov 2014
▼ Oct 2014 ▼ Sep 2014 ▼ Aug 2014
▼ Jul 2014 ▼ Jun 2014 ▼ May 2014

Contents

14 BUSINESS: Streamlining Tour Operators

22 EVENTS : Eco-Conference Venue Selection

17 BUSINESS: SA's Immigration Debacle

25 HOSPITALITY: Thrivability in Green Hotels

EDITORIAL CONTRIBUTORS

Adv. Louis Nel
Andrew Campbell
Dorria Watt
Grant Theis
Jean Francois Mourier

Kagiso Mosue
Kirsten Bohle
Linda Pettit
Lindsay de Heer
Marcelo Risi

Martin Jansen van Vuuren
Nikki Tilley
Raynique Ducie
RJ Friedlander

MAGAZINE SPONSORS

about branding™
your branding is our business

Life is About Branding

DOES YOUR BUSINESS, HOTEL OR TOUR OPERATION STAND OUT FROM THE REST? WHAT MAKES YOU UNIQUE AND VISIBLE?

The breakfast cereal you ate this morning, the car you drove to work, even the mobile phone you made the last call on, was more than just a rational decision. It was most certainly influenced by your brand awareness of the product.

A branded vehicle is a moving billboard attracting the attention of hundreds of new potential customers, while protecting your vehicle against surface damage. No vehicle is too big or too small for branding, and you may opt for something as simple as a company name or as elaborate as a full vehicle wrap. Normal passenger vehicles, panel vans, bakkies, buses, delivery vehicles, school transport and even golf carts qualify for this easy advertising option.

Vehicle branding further extends to the printing of large format digitally printed truck tarpaulins, truck curtains, sign writing on truck curtains and truck covers.

Quote **SATSA** when mailing us to qualify for a 10% discount on your first vehicle wrap.

MORE INFORMATION: Kobus Badenhorst | kobus@aboutbranding.co.za | Cell 082 4491389

Accreditation

Official Travel Trade Journal and Media Partner to:

The African Travel & Tourism Association (Atta)

Tel: +44 20 7937 4408 • Email: info@atta.travel • Website: www.atta.travel

Members in 22 African countries and 37 worldwide use Atta to: Network and collaborate with peers in African tourism; Grow their online presence with a branded profile; Ask and answer specialist questions and give advice; and Attend key industry events.

National Accommodation Association of South Africa (NAA-SA)

Tel: +2786 186 2272 • Fax: +2786 225 9858 • Website: www.naa-sa.co.za

The NAA-SA is a network of mainly smaller accommodation providers around South Africa – from B&Bs in country towns offering comfortable personal service to luxurious boutique city lodges with those extra special touches – you're sure to find a suitable place, and at the same time feel confident that your stay at an NAA-SA member's establishment will meet your requirements.

Regional Tourism Organisation of Southern Africa (RETOSA)

Tel: +2711 315 2420/1 • Fax: +2711 315 2422 • Website: www.retosa.co.za

RETOSA is a Southern African Development Community (SADC) institution responsible for tourism growth and development. RETOSA's aims are to increase tourist arrivals to the region through. RETOSA Member States are Angola, Botswana, DR Congo, Lesotho, Madagascar, Malawi, Mauritius, Mozambique, Namibia, Seychelles, South Africa, Swaziland, Tanzania, Zambia and Zimbabwe.

Southern Africa Tourism Services Association (SATSA)

Tel: +2786 127 2872 • Fax: +2711 886 755 • Website: www.satsa.com

SATSA is a credibility accreditation body representing the private sector of the inbound tourism industry. SATSA members are Bonded thus providing a financial guarantee against advance deposits held in the event of the involuntary liquidation. SATSA represents: Transport providers, Tour Operators, DMC's, Accommodation Suppliers, Tour Brokers, Adventure Tourism Providers, Business Tourism Providers and Allied Tourism Services providers.

Southern African Vehicle Rental and Leasing Association (SAVRALA)

Contact: manager@savrala.co.za • Website: w

Founded in the 1970's, SAVRALA is the representative voice of Southern Africa's vehicle rental, leasing and fleet management sector. Our members have a combined national footprint with more than 600 branches countrywide. SAVRALA are instrumental in steering industry standards and continuously strive to protect both their members' interests, and those of the public, and are therefore widely respected within corporate and government sectors.

Seychelles Hospitality & Tourism Association (SHTA)

Tel: +248 432 5560 • Fax: +248 422 5718 • Website: www.shta.sc

The Seychelles Hospitality and Tourism Association was created in 2002 when the Seychelles Hotel Association merged with the Seychelles Hotel and Guesthouse Association. SHTA's primary focus is to unite all Seychelles tourism industry stakeholders under one association in order to be better prepared to defend the interest of the industry and its sustainability as the pillar of the country's economy.

International Coalition of Tourism Partners (ICTP)

Tel: Haleiwa, USA: +1-808-566-9900 • Cape Town, South Africa: (+27)-21-813-5811 • Rio de Janeiro, Brazil: +5521 40428205 • Germany: +49 2102 1458477 • London, UK: +44 20 3239 3300 • Australia +61 2-8005 1444 • HongKong, China: +852 8120 9450 • Email: member@tourismpartners.org • Website: www.tourismpartners.org

ICTP is a travel and tourism coalition of global destinations committed to Quality Services and Green Growth. ICTP advocates for: sustainable aviation growth; streamlined travel; fair taxation and jobs.

International Institute for Peace through Tourism

Tel: +1-802-253-8671 • Website: www.iipt.org

The International Institute for Peace through Tourism (IIPT) is dedicated to fostering and facilitating tourism initiatives that contribute to international understanding and cooperation, an improved quality of environment, the preservation of heritage, poverty reduction, and the resolution of conflict - and through these initiatives, help bring about a more peaceful and sustainable world.

OTM India 2015

Tel: +9133 4028 4028 • Fax: +9133 2479 0019 • Website: www.otm.co.in

OTM is India's biggest travel trade show, in the largest travel market in India – Mumbai. OTM Mumbai takes place from 4 to 6 February 2015, with an attractive add on option in New Delhi from 10 to 12 February 2015. OTM is the most effective platform to market to the Indian travel industry catering to over 15 million Outbound travellers spending over US$ 10 billion and over 500 million domestic tourists – at least 10% of them with an immediate potential to also travel abroad.

World Travel Market - WTM Africa 2015 - WTM Latin America 2015 - WTM London 20145

WTM Africa takes place in Cape Town, South Africa from 15 to 17 April 2015, WTM Latin America will take place in São Paulo from 22 to 24 April 2015, and WTM - London will take place from 02 to 05 November 2015 in London, England. WTM is the place to do business.

Our cover for May features Hotel Verde Cape Town – 'Africa's Greenest Hotel' – for a while anyway. Because the hotel's owner, Mario Delicio and his industrious team have just launched Verde Hotels – a hospitality solutions group that aims to establish 'Greenest Hotels' in countries throughout Africa, and abroad.

"I had never imagined that my families' humble pursuit to own a green hotel would become the exceptionally caring and inventive establishment that Hotel Verde Cape Town has become. I hope that people will see all of our cumulative efforts and that they will be inspired to implement small changes in their lives and businesses too," says Mario.

And the "small changes" that Mario eludes to are coined in the phrase *'Thrivability'* – meaning the act of thriving and prospering without damaging or causing harm, and encompassing three core concepts: People, Profit and Planet.

Verde Hotel's thrivability model provides sustainable hospitality solutions that meet LEED® certification criteria. The model incorporates responsible design, construction, project and operations management and training. As pioneers in green hospitality globally, Verde Hotels aims to provide socially conscious investors, developers and hoteliers, significantly reduced operating costs and increased profits by providing turnkey service offerings, focused on new commercial construction and retrofitting of existing buildings.

"We believe that thrivability is better suited to the financial and business success of green hospitality than sustainability alone. It is a way to ensure sustainable development while taking the prosperity of one's business model into account, says Samantha Annandale, General Manager of Hotel Verde.

Read more about 'Thrivability in Green Hotel Development' on page 25, and our Property Review feature on Hotel Verde Cape Town on pages 26 to 27.

In fact, this edition of Tourism Tattler has quite a bit of 'Greenery' – from a 'Check List for Eco-Conferencing Venue Selection' (pages 22 to 24), to tips on 'Fostering a Sustainable Hospitality Industry' (page 28).

For Minister Gigaba's (South African Department of Home Affairs) enlightenment, we review UNWTOs Visa Openness Report (page 16), which is in stark contrast to South Africa's Visa Immigration Debacle (page 17).

In addition, we have our usual features, including tourist arrival and hotel stats, ACSA and Car Rental Data (page 12), Louis the Lawyer's 'Law & Contracts' series (page 31) and some marketing tips. **it**

Enjoy your reading!

Yours in Tourism,
Des Langkilde. *editor@tourismtattler.com*

WATCH THE VERDE HOTELS VIDEO

Competition

Win

'Like' / 'Share' / 'Connect' with these Social Media icons to win!

The winning 'Like' or 'Share' during the month of **May 2015** will receive a **Dietz Monarch D10 Hurricane Lantern** with the compliments of **Livingstones Supply Co –** *Suppliers of the Finest Products to the Hospitality Industry*.

Livingston Supply Company

Tourism Tattler

The Dietz Monarch was first introduced in 1900, and has been produced in at least seven distinct variations continuously over the past 108 years. The first and oldest style Monarch had a flat top tank, un-reinforced air tubes, and a 9/16" fuel cap.

Competition Rules: Only one winner will be selected each month on a random selection draw basis. The prize winner will be notified via social media. The prize will be delivered by the sponsor to the winners postal address within South Africa. Should the winner reside outside of South Africa, delivery charges may be applicable. The prize may not be exchanged for cash.

the Safari awards

The 2016 Safari Awards Voting is Now Open

The 2015 Safari Awards Party held in London on 2 November 2014.

Now in its ninth year, there are 18 categories for the 2016 Awards, including two new categories for Best Location and Best Design. To find out more about the property based categories, click here. To find out more about voting in the Safari Awards, including how to vote for wildlife organisatons and the two special personal contribution awards, click here.

The 2016 Safari Awards Categories are:
To view Nominees in each category, just **click on the hyper-linked icon** *next to each category.*

 ### BEST VALUE SAFARI PROPERTY

Cost doesn't always tell the whole story - whether you stayed in one of the higher end lodges, or somewhere more affordable let us know how you thought it did in terms of value for money.

 ### BEST SAFARI CUISINE

Whether it is cooked on a fire, in the bush or in a kitchen, or whether presented in a fine dining room or on the beach around a camp fire, this is your opportunity to rate the food and drink.

 ### BEST NEW SAFARI PROPERTY

This category is aimed at new properties which have opened within the last three years - let us know how you think they are doing.

 ### BEST RIDING SAFARI

As well as mobile safaris or the traditional game drive on four wheels, there are several specialist operators offering riding safaris on horseback.

 ### BEST MARINE SAFARI EXPERIENCE

Many lodges based near the coast or large lakes can offer a rnge of marine based activities. If you opted for one such lodge, let us know how their activities faired.

 ### BEST ECOLOGICALLY RESPONSIBLE SAFARI PROPERTY

Consider what the property does to protect the natural ecology as well as the local flora and fauna. How well does the property do in regards to minimizing its environmental impact and reducing its use of non-renewable energy?

 ### BEST FAMILY SAFARI EXPERIENCE

If you stayed at a lodge that considers itself family friendly, let us know how well you think they delivered for the kids.

 ### BEST WALKING SAFARI

Walking safaris are a great way to view things from a different perspective to the typical game drive on four wheels.

 ### BEST SAFARI SPA / RETREAT

Many lodges now offer, or even specialise in, spa treatments to add an extra bit of luxury to your trip. Let us know how much you enjoyed being pampered on your safari.

 ### MOST ROMANTIC SAFARI PROPERTY

For many a safari trip is a trip of a lifetime - and when better to make that trip than on honeymoon or for a special anniversary. If you were looking for a bit of romance on your trip, let us know how well your lodge scored with all things romantic.

 ### BEST COMMUNITY FOCUSED SAFARI PROPERTY

How well does the property integrate with and provide support for the local communities? Do communities benefit financially or in other ways from the property?

 ### BEST SAFARI HOUSE

In addition to lodges or tented accommodation, safari houses are increasingly popular. If that was your chosen accommodation type, rate it in this category.

 ### BEST MOBILE SAFARI

Mobile safaris are a popular choice - let us know if it lived up to your expectations.

 ### BEST SAFARI GUIDING TEAM

Wildlife is a huge part of going on safari, so its crucial to have expert guides who can get you as close to the action as possible. Use this category to rate the guides at the lodge you stayed at.

 ### BEST WILDLIFE CONSERVATION ORGANISATION

This award recognises the best wildlife conservation organisations.

 ### BEST CHARITY

This award recognises the best charitable organisations.

 ### BEST PERSONAL CONTRIBUTION TO WILDLIFE CONSERVATION

The first of two two special awards for outstanding individuals goes to someone in the field of Wildlife Conservation.

 ### BEST PERSONAL CONTRIBUTION TO TOURISM

The second of two two special awards for outstanding individuals goes to someone in the field of safari Tourism.

For more information visit: http://www.safariawards.com/

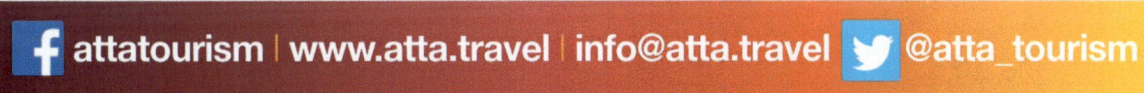

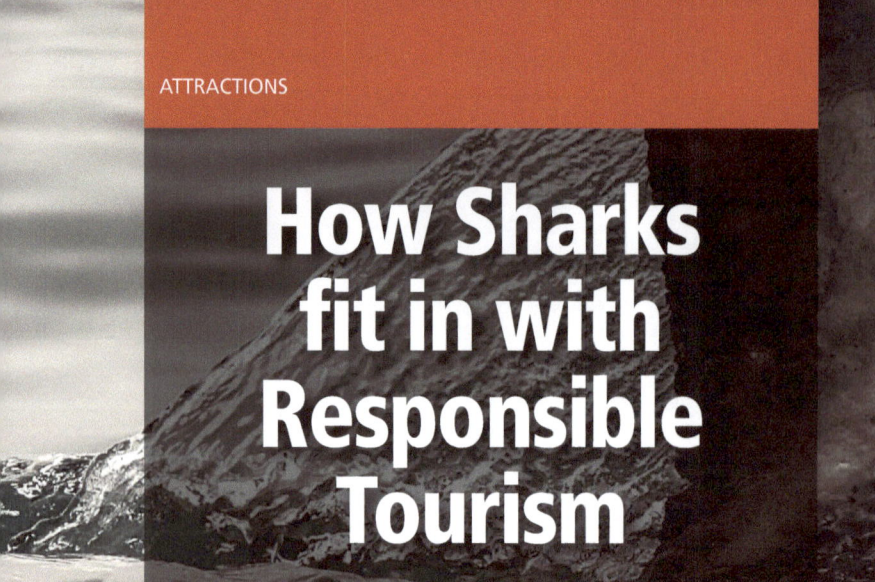

How Sharks fit in with Responsible Tourism

It's hard to imagine how Great White Sharks fit in with responsible tourism practices, but that's exactly what a South African tour operating company has accomplished over the past 24 years, writes **Des Langkilde**.

South Africa is acknowledged as being a destination with an abundance of white sharks *(Carcharodon carcharias)* off its coastline, and both domestic and international tourists flock to areas such as Mossel Bay, Gansbaai and False Bay to experience them as an adrenalin filled "Bucket List" encounter.

The Department of Environmental Affairs and Tourism (DEAT) is tasked with the management of the cage diving industry in South Africa. As such, operational procedures and the industries compliance all fall under DEAT's mandate. The Marine Living Resources Act (MLRA), was ratified in 1998 (Act No. 18, 1998), seven years after vessels in South Africa began to attract white sharks for tourism and viewing purposes, while national legislation protecting all shark species was passed in 1991. The MLRA had to assess several considerations, including the development of international tourism, socio-economic considerations, and the optimal sustainable utilisation of South Africa's marine resources. As such, it was decided that the existing industry fulfilled the MLRA's mandate with regards to the non-consumptive exploitation of the protected white shark.

The most crucial of these operational stipulations (in regard to links between cage diving and shark attacks at nearby bathing beaches) were concerned with limiting cage dive activities to seal islands where natural chumming occurs, and forbidding of any intentional feeding of sharks. Within these and other regulatory confines, DEAT is satisfied they have fulfilled their role in applying the MLR's act in a responsible, informed and cautious manner with regard to the industries management.

Critics of the industry, however, point out that in addition to 'optimal utilisation' the MLRA also stipulates the need to apply a precautionary approach in respect of the management and development of marine living resources. To minimize ecological and behavioural impacts 'Permit Conditions' and a 'Code of Conduct' have been established.

The regulatory reliance of 'voluntarily buy in' by operators has recently been enhanced through the Department of Tourism tasking the Southern Africa Tourism Sevices Association (SATSA) to manage compliance in the adventure tourism sector.

Ultimately compliance will benefit the industry, the white sharks conservation status, and most importantly satisfy tourism demand for shark cage diving experiences in a responsible manner.

As a SATSA member, White Shark Projects (WSP) is a prime example of how sharks fit in with responsible tourism practices. WSP was founded in 1990 as a research and conservation enterprise, and are the financial partner to the South African Shark Conservancy, who research not only white sharks but also other shark species. Fully committed to responsible tourism practices, WSP not only supports the preservation and protection of sharks but also to the growth and upliftment of local communities and the environment in which they operate.

Staff are recruited locally and ongoing training ensures that they remain up skilled and motivated. Employment means they are able to play a positive role in the economy, are able to provide for their families and have a 25% ownership of the company through the WSP Employees Trust.

WSP also conduct tourism and environmental education programmes in Gansbaai schools, which fosters pride and a personal sense of responsibility towards the environment. A flagship White Shark Projects Recycle Swop Shop has been running successfully for over 6 years. On average 85 children visit the swop shop a week and interact with staff and volunteers thus bridging the gap between cultures and communities. A soup kitchen is also held on Swop Shop Days. **it**

For more information visit www.whitesharkprojects.co.za

Read more articles on the subject of sharks via these links:
Great White Shark Behaviour
South Africa's Great White Sharks
Extreme Adventure: White Shark Diving
Shark Research on the Whale Coast

Interview:

Kuoni Group

interact | inspire | engage

If you want your tourism product to be taken seriously, and considered for inclusion by one of the world's largest B2B wholesalers and online providers of hotel accommodation and land services, you'd better take Responsible Tourism seriously, writes **Des Langkilde**.

During the 11th International Conference on Responsible Tourism in Destinations (RTD11) event held in Cape Town prior to, and during WTM-Africa, I met with **Matthias Leisinger**, Vice President or Corporate Responsibility at Kuoni Travel Holdings Ltd, and asked him some pertinent questions relating to Africa inbound services.

But before I go into the interview, here's some background information on the Kuoni Group:

Kuoni Group is a global service provider to the travel industry, founded in 1906 in Zurich, Switzerland. Today Kuoni Group has operations in more than 100 countries on five continents, and will employ around 8 000 people (FTE) in its future organisation. Kuoni Group focuses on three core activities:

- Global B2B wholesaler and online provider of hotel accommodation and land services.
- Destination services from accommodation, transportation, tours and activities, to venues and event management.
- Industry pioneer and world's leading visa services provider. Works for 45 governments and operates 1 486 Application Centres in 120 countries.
- Kuoni Group's turnover for the 2014 financial year came to 5 508 million CHF (Swiss Francs - about US$5.76m or ZAR69,17m).
- In 2014 13.6 million hotel room nights were booked through Kuoni in GTD division – an increase of 7.1% against the previous year. Around 38'000 room nights were booked per day online.
- In Global Travel Services (GTS) division around 50'000 group tours were organized with 3.1 million booked room nights. In addition Kuoni Group's global network of nine Destination Management Specialists served 738'000 customers with destination services in 2014.
- Visa services provider VFS Global processed 18.2 million visa applications worldwide and almost 6 million biometric data sets were recorded for its government clients in 2014.
- Kuoni ranks among the top five tour operators in Europe.
- Following the decision to focus the company's activities on its core business as a service provider to the global travel industry and to governments, the Board of Directors and the Group Executive Board decided in January to divest its tour operating activities. Kuoni Group intends to find new owners for its tour operating activities during the course of 2015.

Enough already! If you want more info on Kuoni Group, browse their website at *www.kuoni.com*. Back to the interview, I (**it**) asked Matthias Leisinger (**ML**):

it: How does Kuoni work with Africa inbound products?

ML: "*Private Safaris* is a subsidiary of Kuoni, with offices in Kenya, Namibia, Tanzania (Arusha and Zanzibar) and South Africa, who are responsible for product sourcing and development in Africa, and will be exhibiting at Indaba 2015 in Durban." (*May 9-11, on stand ICCE12 – to book an appointment go to www.privatesafaris.com/ indaba-2015-meeting-calendar/*).

it: Any niche products in demand?

ML: "There is increasing demand for fair trade travel products. However, the source markets are often not aware of the responsible tourism products or projects that are available in Africa, as many are not at the right level of maturity to meet Kuoni's requirements in terms of service standards."

it: And what are the fair trade travel requirements?

ML: "All components of the package (tour operator, transport, activities and accommodation) as well as all contractual relationships in the value chain have to be audited against Fair Trade standards by an independent auditing company. The auditing company is *Fair Trade Tourism* (FTT) in Africa, and the standards are designed to ensure that workers and affected communities benefit from tourism through long-term trading relationships, full prepayment and binding cancellation agreements. In addition, a fair trade premium (5% of the package cost) is channelled into a central fund and used for development projects in Africa."

So there you have it! If you want your tourism product to be taken seriously adopt *Responsible Tourism Practices*, and get *Fair Trade Tourism* certified.   **it**

About Matthias Leisinger: *Matthias is a specialist in corporate social responsibility (CSR) and sustainable tourism with 13 years of experience in the private sector. His professional goal is driving change to create a more sustainable business model. He has a record of success in creating and implementing corporate sustainability strategy and initiatives including human rights due diligence, supply chain management, stakeholder management and reporting. He speakes at various events and conferences, and is experienced in planning, developing and implementing responsible tourism projects in various countries.*

SATSA
Southern Africa Tourism Services Association

Grant Thornton

B⊘NDED*

Market Intelligence Report

The information below was extracted from data available as at **24 April 2015**. By **Martin Jansen van Vuuren** of **Grant Thornton**.

ARRIVALS

The latest available data from **Statistics South Africa** is for **January to December 2014***:

	Current period	Change over same period last year
UK	401 914	3.50%
Germany	274 571	10.22%
USA	309 255	5.02%
India	85 639	-8.49%
China (incl Hong Kong)	82 905	-24.66%
Total Overseas Arrivals	2 254 709	2.92%

HOTEL STATS

The latest available data from **STR Global** is for **February 2015**:

Current period	Average Room Occupancy (ARO)	Average Room Rate (ARR)	Revenue Per Available Room (RevPAR)
All Hotels in SA	61.1%	R 1 148	R 701
All 5-star hotels in SA	64.9%	R 2 120	R 1 377
All 4-star hotels in SA	61.4%	R 1 079	R 662
All 3-star hotels in SA	58.8%	R 872	R 513
Change over same period last year			
All Hotels in SA	-2.4%	6.0%	3.5%
All 5-star hotels in SA	-2.3%	7.3%	4.9%
All 4-star hotels in SA	-1.9%	6.0%	4.0%
All 3-star hotels in SA	-5.1%	7.8%	2.3%

ACSA DATA

The latest available data from **ACSA** is for **January to March 2014**:

Change over same period last year	Passengers arriving on International Flights	Passengers arriving on Regional Flights	Passengers arriving on Domestic Flights
OR Tambo International	-0.6%	-1.1%	5.5%
Cape Town International	8.3%	-0.6%	5.4%
King Shaka International	5.1%	N/A	3.0%

CAR RENTAL DATA

The latest available data from **SAVRALA** is for **January to December 2014**:

	Current period	Change over same period last year
Industry rental days	15 888 314	-0.2%
Industry utilisation	69.1%	-2.1%
Industry Average daily revenue	4 891 660 507	5%

WHAT THIS MEANS FOR MY BUSINESS

Indications are that business tourism is growing. STR Global data indicate that hotel occupancies are stabilising while average room rates are continuing to improve. Business travellers are more likely to pay higher rates that leisure travellers.

ACSA data is showing that domestic travel is recovering but that arrivals on international flights to South Africa's main airport has declined. Leisure travellers on international flights are more likely to have been discouraged by Ebola and visa regulations while business travellers on domestic flights would still need to travel for business purposes.

*Statistics South Africa has stopped counting people transiting through South Africa as tourists. As a result of the revision, in order to compare the 2014 figures with 2013, it has been necessary to deduct the transit figures from the 2013 totals.

i**t**

For more information contact Martin at Grant Thornton on +27 (0)21 417 8838 or visit: http://www.gt.co.za

Tourism Business Performance Steady in Q1 2015

Amid calls for calm in various parts of the country, which have seen an upsurge of violence against foreign nationals, first quarter results of the TBCSA Tourism Business Index ("TBI") show that business performance in the travel and tourism industry remained steady in the first three months of 2015, writes **Kagiso Mosue**.

TBCSA FNB Tourism Business Index

1st Quarter 2015 Results

18th Edition – 1st Quarter 2015 Results   April 2015

TBI is a performance monitoring tool aimed at providing regular, up-to-date information on the performance of tourism businesses, including an outlook of performance over the next three months.

Commenting on the latest TBI report, TBCSA Chief Executive Officer, Ms. Mmatšatši Ramawela said although she was pleased with the steady performance, the Council was mindful of the lower performance level score achieved in this quarter and concerned about the impact of the negative publicity generated by the latest flare of violence against foreign nationals on the travel and tourism trade.

"Whilst we are pleased with the reported steady performance and TBI score of 99.9, our overall review of performance levels recorded over the past two years is showing concerning signs of a possible slowdown in tourism business activity. This does not come as a surprise to us given the challenges in the operating environment including the lingering effect of the Ebola outbreak and the introduction of the new immigration regulations. The situation has been further exacerbated by the current uncertainties over energy supply by Eskom. The recent spate of 'xenophobic attacks' on foreign nationals in various parts of the country are also likely to add fuel to the fire, impacting on South Africa's reputation as an attractive tourist destination", Ramawela said

Delving deeper into the report, a slightly better picture emerges for the Accommodation business segment, which experienced better than normal business performance with an index score of 110.2 compared to the forecast score of 101.9. The Other Tourism Businesses segment (excluding accommodation performed somewhat less than normal at 92.1 compared to the forecast score of 102.7.)

In this quarter, TBI recorded a strong response rate for the car rental companies who registered lower performance than in the last quarter of 2014. This performance was also much lower than forecast. Marc Corcoran, President of the Southern African Vehicle Rental and Leasing Association (SAVRALA) said this *"is likely to be due to the increased vehicle pricing starting to come through and the pressure to obtain the required price increases. The car rental industry however remains optimistic going forward."*

"What is encouraging though is that for the year ahead both sectors on balance expect a better than normal performance with a high positive balance of 37% from the accommodation sector" says Gillian Saunders, Head of Advisory at Grant Thornton.

"This also translates into the strong capacity growth expectations for the next quarter similar to what we have seen from the accommodation sector for seven consecutive TBIs, peaking at high levels in the last two quarters. Sadly though this is not translating as strongly into job creation as the accommodation sector is actually slightly negative on balance for job creation in the next quarter. Accommodation businesses are fighting the impact of other increased business operating costs such as rates and electricity by maximising labour productivity", adds Saunders.

Through the TBI, the TBCSA has continued to monitor private sector sentiment on two key developments affecting the sector – the impact of the Ebola outbreak in three West African countries and the ongoing issues relating to South Africa's introduction of new immigration regulations.

"On the impact of the Ebola outbreak, what is coming through quite strongly from business is that more could have been done from a PR point of view to address the negative perceptions and ignorance about the geography of the African continent. This is a key lesson we must learn from this painful experience", explains Ramawela.

With the deadline of 1 June looming for the Department of Home Affairs' implementation of the new immigration regulation regarding travelling with minors, the Other Tourism Businesses segment (59,3% of respondents) proves to be more prone to the negative impact of the requirement for unabridged birth certificates compared to the Accommodation business segment (24,5% of respondents). Twenty-five percent (25%) of all respondents say they have had a somewhat negative impact to their business as a result of the pending introduction of the unabridged birth certificates.

"Even with the slightly more pessimistic outlook going into the next quarter (with an index score of 97.3), we remain positive. We are pleased to see Government taking such a strong stance on the issue of the 'xenophobic attacks' and moving quickly to arrest perpetrators of these violent acts. Unfortunately, the social media has also been used by some as a tool to provoke and instigate violence and we hope the police will move swiftly to address this as well. As the TBCSA we will continue to liaise with our counterparts in Government and communicate any updates with members and the broader travel and tourism trade. What is key is to focus on ensuring that stability returns in the operating environment", Ramawela said.

The full TBI Q1 report can be downloaded HERE.

How to streamline your Tour Operator business

Surprisingly, there are still tour operators who rely on manual (spreadsheet and other) solutions to run their businesses, which invariably leads to costly errors, resource wastage and loss of business due to the slow turnaround time in getting quotes to prospective clients. In this article, **Lindsay de Heer** explains how to use software to streamline your tour operator business.

Letting go of your existing office workflow processes, is a bit like having someone else pack your kitchen cupboards. That feeling of not having control, not being able to find anything and trying many doors before finding what you are looking for can be daunting.

But what if the reordering of your kitchen actually meant that you spent less time there? What if it improved your workflow and you spent less time going back and forth between your appliances? What if you enjoyed your new space so much, that it inspired you to be more creative and productive?

How does this analogy translate to tour operator software? Simple. Tour operator software can reorganise your workflow, ensuring that you save time, improve accuracy and eliminate any unnecessary processes.

A purpose designed tour operator software solution looks at the core principles of your business requirements; • Fast • Accurate • Efficient • User Friendly • Client facing documentation • Reporting functionality.

So if there are so many benefits to moving to a software solution, why is the change still so daunting? Well, let's go back to the kitchen analogy again; if you take time to open each cupboard, see how things have been repacked, move between each appliance, and locate your most importance utensils, you are already 90% of the way to becoming aware of your new space.

By way of example, let's look at **Travelogic™**, which was established more than 10 years ago by working closely with industry professionals. Travelogic offers a full, detailed demonstration of the software, which includes a step-by-step overview of what the software can do to improve your current business process and to ensure that it is the right fit for your needs.

The heart of tour operator software is the database of suppliers. Each supplier needs to be set up with all the relevant details, including and most importantly, the rate rules, rates and supplier content. This can be a time consuming task that can be overwhelming for a first time user. Travelogic has a team of experienced database managers, who are able to load this information on your behalf, giving you the benefit of experience and accuracy.

Full training is given on all aspects of the software system. From product managers to consultants; accountants to business owners. An experienced support team assists with queries once you start using the programme. The support team have an in-depth knowledge of the product, and are able to help you when you can't find that all important tool (utensil), when navigating the system. A user manual

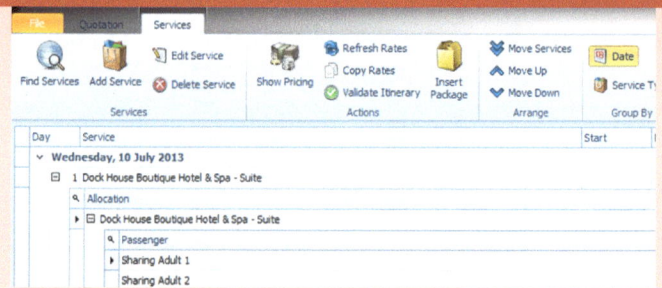

A screenshot of Travelogic's tour operator itinerary feature.

is also provided to refer to as well as an online help centre to answer your FAQ's.

From Travelogic you will be able to manage your request from Quotation to Voucher. You can produce a quote (including pictures and content), put together an itinerary, pull an invoice and collate a voucher, all within the system.

If you are looking for a more dynamic Itinerary output, Travelogic have partnered with Smartbox, who will design a template to your specifications, while Travelogic provides the link required in order for the data to sit on this document output.

You use Wetu? No problem; integration is provided to ensure that all your suppliers are mapped to a Wetu point and just like that you are able to include Wetu maps and data on a Travelogic itinerary or vice versa.

Want access to Live Availability? No problem; the software integrates with companies such as ResRequest and Nightsbridge to allow a link to live availability and rates through Travelogic.

The beauty of technology means that we can assist any operator around the world. The product can be accessed anywhere, anytime and if you don't have your own server, Travelogic can host one for you; offering a maintained and monitored solution.

Still afraid to take the plunge? That's okay; Travelogic have done this before, and are on hand to offer advice and guidance through the implementation process. Their experienced management team and skilled developers are here to ensure that your move from a manual to a software solution is as smooth and stress-free as possible. **it**

For more information visit *www.travelogic.co.za*

*Read more on **'How to keep itineraries current'** in the March 2015 edition of the Tourism Tattler Trade Journal (pages 11-13) or read the online feature article at www.tourismtattler.com/?p=58834.*

Governments recognise benefits of visa facilitation

" Governments should extend to the maximum number of countries the practice of abolishing, through bilateral agreements or by unilateral decision, the requirement of entry visas for temporary visitors. "

Declaration at the 1963 United Nations Conference on International Travel and Tourism in Rome, and attended by delegates of 87 States, including South Africa.

Visa facilitation has experienced strong progress in recent years, particularly through the implementation of visa on arrival policies according to UNWTO's Visa Openness Report. This largely reflects an increased awareness among policymakers of the positive impacts of visa facilitation on tourism and economic growth, writes **Marcelo Risi**.

According to the Report, 62% of the world's population required a traditional visa prior to departure in 2014, down from 77% in 2008. In the same year, 19% of the world's population was able to enter a destination without a visa, while 16% could receive a visa on arrival, as compared to 17% and 6% in 2008.

The Report also shows that the most prevalent facilitation measure implemented has been 'visa on arrival'. Over half of all improvements made in the last four years were from 'visa required' to 'visa on arrival' requirements.

"Visa facilitation is central to stimulating economic growth and job creation through tourism. Although there is much room for improvement, we are pleased to see that a growing number of governments around the world are taking decisive steps in this regard", said UNWTO Secretary-General, Taleb Rifai.

Countries in the Americas and in Asia and the Pacific have been at the forefront of visa facilitation, while Europe and Middle East have more restrictive visa policies. Overall, emerging economies tend to be more open than advanced ones, with South-East Asia, East Africa, the Caribbean and Oceania among the most open subregions.

"UNWTO forecasts international tourist arrivals to reach 1.8 billion by 2030, and easier visa procedures will be crucial to attract these travellers, especially tourists from emerging source markets like China, Russia, India and Brazil", added Mr Rifai.

Research by UNWTO and the World Travel and Tourism Council (WTTC) shows that the G20 economies could boost their international tourist numbers by an additional 122 million, generate an extra US$ 206 billion in tourism exports and create over five million additional jobs by improving visa processes and entry formalities. The same research carried out for the APEC and the ASEAN countries indicates that visa facilitation could generate important gains for both groups, including the creation of 2.6 million jobs in APEC and 650.000 jobs in ASEAN.

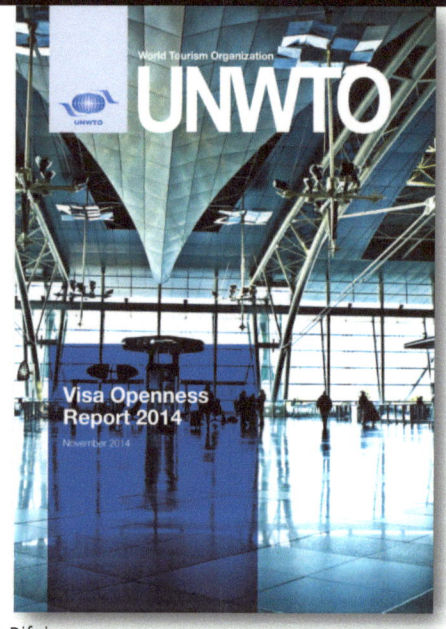

The functions of visas

Visa policies are among the most important governmental formalities influencing tourism internationally. The development of policies and procedures for visas, as well as for other important travel documents such as passports, is closely linked to the development of tourism. With the swift growth of international tourism in the last six decades, the quality, reliability, and functionality of visas and other travel documents has evolved. Only half a century ago, travel was heavily impacted by customs regulations, currency exchange limitations and visa formalities.

A great deal of progress has been made in facilitation, which has contributed to the remarkable growth of the tourism sector. Especially noteworthy are the multilateral agreements that mutually exempt all or certain categories of travellers from the visa requirement. However, despite the progress made, namely in recent years, current visa policies are still often inadequate and inefficient, and are thus acknowledged to be an obstacle to tourism growth.

Travellers mainly see visas as a formality that imposes a cost. If the cost of obtaining a visa – either the direct monetary cost imposed in the form of fees or the indirect costs, which can include distance, time spent waiting in lines, and the complexity of the process – exceeds a threshold, potential travellers are simply deterred from making a particular journey or choose an alternative destination with less hassle.

To download the 'UNESCO Visa Openness Report 2014' click here.

About the author: Marcelo Risi is the Senior Media Officer at the United Nations World Tourism Organisation (UNWTO). Data on visa policies by country is collected by UNWTO on an annual basis since 2008 and validated through surveys and communication with the Organization's Member States.

South Africa's Visa Immigration Debacle Rages on

The visa requirement for unabridged birth certificates for minors entering South Africa are due to come into effect on 01 June 2015, and the Southern Africa Tourism Services Association (SATSA) is appealing to the inbound travel trade to unite and demand that the birth certificate requirements be abolished in their entirety, writes **Des Langkilde**.

"The visa regulations are being imposed without due consideration of our sector and will result in significant losses to our industry. Firstly, we are the only country in the world following this (birth certificate) path and there are far more sophisticated, multi-agency measures that are required to tackle the scourge of child trafficking, which, by the way, is not a major security threat! Secondly, we appreciate the need for enhanced security with respect to biometric data, but this could best be captured on arrival. This will be far more cost effective and will not have the devastating effect on tourism numbers we have already witnessed out of China and India," says David Frost, CEO of the Southern Africa Tourism Services Association (SATSA).

Reflecting on the beleaguered process involved in dealing with the South African Department of Home Affairs to date, Frost cites the following actions:

March 2014

- Regulations gazetted in the Government Gazette (missed by everyone in tourism – including South Africa's own Tourism Ministry and Department).

June 2014

- Regulations formally announced.
(Read more: 'SA Tourism Minister Broaches Immigration Debacle' Editor).

July 2014

- The Tourism Business Council of South Africa (TBCSA) and other key stakeholders write to Minister Gigaba requesting a meeting – receipt of letters acknowledged – but no response.
- TBCSA commissions a Grant Thornton report on potential impact of regulations.
- Minister Hanekom meets with Minister Gigaba, resulting in a joint press statement stating there will be no need for supporting documentation or translations of birth certificates.

September 2014

- Meeting secured with Minister of Home Affairs by CEO SATSA – leads to meeting with Minister Gigaba early October. Grant Thorton report presented – no response to the report at all to date.
(Read more: 'New South African Visa Regulations Postponed' Editor).

October 2014

- Minister Gigaba announces postponement of implementation of birth certificates until 1st June 2015 and establishment of a tourism task force to look into the implementation of the regulations.

- No formal meeting of the task force – although TBCSA secures informal meeting with DDG of Home Affairs.
- Minister Gigaba reneges on deal struck with Minister Hanekom and now official copy of birth certificates as well as supporting documentation required.
(Read more: 'TBCSA Immigration Report Leaked' Editor).

February 2015

- State of the Nation address – President Zuma announces a review to balance interests of tourism and security.

March 2015

- Official stats released show 50% drop from China in last four months of 2014 and 15% drop from India – directly attributable to threat of implementation of in-person biometric visa applications.
(Read more: 'SA Tourism Stats finally released' Editor).

April 2015

- No review process clarified yet, despite letters requesting this from TBCSA.
- TBCSA commissions new Grant Thornton report (quantifying actual damage and reviewing international best practice that does not harm tourism).

"In summary – in a fully functioning democracy, despite numerous requests and letters, the tourism sector, which represents 9% of South Africa's economy, has not been able to table its position on any of these regulations with Home Affairs in the year since the process began. We have been actively snubbed by Home Affairs and when interaction has occurred it has been with no debate, discussion nor ability to raise our concerns. The fabled task team announced by Minister Gigaba has never been formally convened despite ongoing pressure from TBCSA.

We have, through this process, forged a close working relationship with our Minister Hanekom and his senior team and NDT and SA Tourism. He is fundamentally opposed to the regulations in their current form and is working through the Economics Cluster within Cabinet. We will continue to oppose these damaging moves by Home Affairs," concludes Frost.

Diarise the date: The **2015 SATSA Conference** will take place at Fancourt in George from **13th – 15th August** this year.

Rhino Conservation Awards Honour Rangers

Game rangers are the soldiers on the frontlines in the war against the desecration of a species, putting their lives and that of their families on the line for nature conservation, writes **Andrew Campbell** of the Game Ranger's Association of Africa (GRAA).

Lawrence Munro, winner of the Best Conservation Practitioner Rhino Conservation Award in 2014, previously the head ranger of the iMfolozi wilderness area in the southern section of Hluhluwe-iMfolozi Park, now heads up the Rhino Operations Unit, the anti-poaching task force for the whole of KwaZulu-Natal. Munro's unit has been relatively successful and he attributes much of the success to targeting poachers and their syndicates outside of protected areas, rather than waiting for poachers to come into the reserves.

A great advance in the war against poaching is the listing of rhino poaching as a priority national crime, indicating that government's intelligence and security agencies now support conservation agencies.

This essential yet dangerous line of work is unforgiving, unrelenting and dangerous. Thirty-nine year-old Munro, who has a young family, is constantly armed and on guard. *"I am thinking combatively all the time,"* he explains. *"My family and I have had very directed, pointed death threats. Letters addressed to me that say: we don't want you around anymore."*

The implications of his line of work mean that his family cannot travel after dark without Munro acting as escort; he works strenuously long hours – preparing in the day and hunting poachers at night. This places stress on his family and affects every facet of his life. Munro is often forced to keep a lot of his work secret, unwilling to reveal anything to his family that will endanger their lives. Despite the danger, Munro loves his work. "It's such a great feeling to catch a rhino poacher or middleman. But the job does take its toll."

Nominations are open for the Rhino Conservation Awards 2015 and are invited from all African rhino range states, in categories including; Best Field Ranger, Best Conservation Practitioner, Best Political and Judicial Support, Best Science Research and Technology, and Best Awareness, Education or Funding. The additional Special Youths category honours youngsters that have taken action against poaching.

Nominations close on 01 June 2015 and can be made by or on behalf of any person or organisation that has played a part in rhino conservation, on any scale. Nomination forms can be requested from Janyce Dalziel at *janyce@currintevents.co.za*, or downloaded from the Rhino Awards website: *www.rhinoconservationawards.org*. **it**

Rhino Poaching Deaths vs Poacher Arrests - Stats for South Africa by Province

Year	2010		2011		2012		2013		2014		2015	
Deaths vs Arrests	Deaths	Arrests	Deaths	Arrests	Deaths	Arrests	Deaths	Arrests	Deaths	Arrests	Deaths	Arrests
KNP (SanParks)	146	67	252	82	425	73	606	133	827	174	29	09
MNP (SanParks)	00	00	06	00	03	00	03	00	00	00	00	00
MAP (SanParks)	00	00	00	00	00	00	00	00	01	01	00	00
Gauteng	15	10	03	16	01	26	08	10	05	21	00	00
Limpopo	52	36	80	34	59	43	114	34	110	60	12	00
Mpumalanga	17	16	31	73	28	66	92	00	83	45	02	04
North West	57	02	31	21	77	32	87	70	65	14	00	03
Eastern Cape	04	07	11	02	07	00	05	26	15	02	00	00
Free State	03	00	04	00	00	06	04	07	04	00	00	00
KwaZulu-Natal	38	25	34	04	66	20	85	63	99	68	06	01
Western Cape	00	02	06	00	02	00	00	00	01	01	00	00
Northern Cape	01	00	00	00	00	01	00	00	05	00	00	00
TOTAL	333	165	448	232	668	267	1004	343	1215	386	49	17

KNP = Kruger National Park, MNP = Mpumalanga National Park, MAP = Mapungubwe National Park. Statistics released by the DEAT as at 22 January 2015.

Incidents of poaching can be reported to the anonymous tip-off lines 0800 205 005, 08600 10111 or Crime-Line on 32211.

Call for China to Support Africa Conservation

Following our article **'Taking Responsible Tourism to China'** in the April edition, **Dorria Watt** follows up with the outcome on Deborah Calmeyer's presentation to guests at the prestigious 'Her Village International Forum' in Beijing, China.

So strong was the call for support for the closure of all ivory and rhino horn trade into Africa at a high profile Forum in Beijing that a Resolution was co-signed by host Yang Lan, Wang Shi, Dereck and Beverly Joubert and ROAR AFRICA CEO, Deborah Calmeyer. Environmental lobby groups WildAid China and SEE also signed the Resolution. The Forum, attended by 400 top business men and women, with a TV broadcast to another 200 million viewers, had Africa's elephants and rhinos as one of its key topics.

Calmeyer's speech, entitled 'The Final Hour', highlighted the need for global assistance to preserve Africa's natural resources. "*We are losing our key animals,' she said, 'and along with them a part of our humanity. Elephant, rhino and lions are in their final hour without them, the eco-tourism industry into Africa will fail and entire communities will perish.*

'It's true that Africa is a harsh place but it is also a place of incredible beauty, ingenuity, growth, happiness and warmth and whether we value these animals right to live or their role in our ecosystem, we cannot ignore the massive tragedy of the decimation of these species."

She presented three hard-hitting figures in terms of the economic value of tourism and how all of it could change, especially for Africa, if we are unable to protect and sustain our wildlife. In Southern Africa, nature-based tourism generates roughly the same revenue as farming, forestry and fisheries combined.

- 8 million is the number of visits to the world's national parks and nature reserves, generating 3.7 trillion RMB (7.2 trillion ZAR). Yet only 62 billion RMB (121 million ZAR) is used to conserve these areas.

- 277 million. That's the number of people in employment supported by travel and tourism in 2014. This means 1 in 11 of all jobs in the world are from tourism.

- 47 trillion RMB (92 trillion ZAR) is the total contribution made by travel and tourism to the global economy last year – growing the global economy by 9.8%. In 2014 tourism grew faster than any other of the big sectors in the world economy.

"*With tourism into Africa from China on the rise the fate of our rhino, elephants and lion is as much in your hands as the people of Africa,' she said. 'In the spirit of the Year of the Goat – a symbol of benevolence, promise and prosperity - and the Year of China in South Africa, it is critical we join forces to take action. We need more durable solutions that ban the trade of endangered wildlife products, we need to close the markets and persuade consumers to stop buying these products.*

'We know the kind of tactics that work and these are education, persuasion and government action. As Africans we need to take the primary responsibility for solving the poaching crisis but we also need the help of China. Together with China we believe we can make a difference and ensure endangered species have a future. To quote WildAid: When the buying stops the killing can too."

The co-signed Resolution contained the following summation: *We as consumers are awakening and taking action; to refuse to consume elephant tusk, rhino horn or other endangered wild animal products; to reduce and cut off the demand for such products, breaking the chain of profit, in order to protect endangered species.*

The Forum is a powerful vehicle for change and Bradley Brouwer, President: Asia Pacific, South African Tourism said: "*We are inspired by one of South Africa's influential female talents in tourism, Deborah Calmeyer, CEO of ROAR AFRICA speaking at the inspiring and very successful 'Her Village International Forum' and presenting the diversified resources available in South Africa. South Africa is sought after by global travellers credited to its breathtaking scenic beauty, various wildlife, dynamic cultures and stunning adventures. China has become one of the core source-markets for South Africa since 2014. With the arrival of 2015 as the 'Year of China in South Africa', South African Tourism has embraced the remarkable developmental opportunities presented.*"

The final word goes to Confucius: 'As the crown of creation, each of us has a responsibility to support and participate in activities to protect the earth, protect endangered wildlife, and protect our homes and children's future! '

For more information visit www.roarafrica.com

Seychelles Biggest Event a Success

For decades the Seychelles has seen activities and events being organized but never before has one event captured the imagination of the people of Seychelles and earned their support.

The launch of the Carnaval International de Victoria five years ago captivated the Seychelles public from the outset, and support for this event has grown annually making it the biggest event ever organized in Seychelles.

"The proof of the pudding is in the eating. The Ministry of Tourism and Culture and its Tourism Board has managed to stage an event that clearly appeals to the Seychellois Community and they have continued to show their support for the three days of the carnival event by being out and about in Victoria," said Alain St.Ange, the Seychelles Minister responsible for Tourism and Culture.

At the 2015 edition of the island's carnival Minister Alain St.Ange, accompanied by Sherin Naiken, the CEO of the Tourism Board, Anne Lafortune, the PS for Tourism and Benjamine Rose, the PS for Culture led the first part of the carnival procession themselves. As the main organizers of the event that has captured the Seychelles they were seen at the front of the parade waving to the large crowd who had gathered alongside the carnival route.

"We all feel good at the Ministry and at the Tourism Board because we have managed to stage an event that the Seychellois want, that they appreciate and that they support with their heart. The opening ceremony is popular, the carnival parade continues to see the Seychellois gather in Victoria to such a degree that it is now over flowing with people and the carnival closing ceremony is today recognized as the only event that manages to fill 'Freedom Square' to capacity in the centre of Victoria. The text messages, emails and letters we continue to receive year after year shows clearly that what we are doing is appreciated. It shows that our efforts are being well received by the people of Seychelles," Minister St.Ange added.

The carnival in Seychelles has grown to become listed as a world class event on the Community of Nations events calendar. The Press Community continues to be supportive of this carnival that brings to life a 'Melting Pot of Cultures' and has subsequently been baptized as the 'Carnival of Carnivals'.

Predicting the ongoing success of the event, the editor of Tourism Tattler, Des Langkilde wrote about the 2013 event; *"Judging by the increased popularity of this cultural extravaganza over the past three years, the Carnaval International de Victoria is set to become one of the 'must see' annual events in the international tourism calendar."*

St.Ange says that the carnival is a unique world event for bringing nations together where different cultures are respected as well as

celebrated. *"Even in the General Assembly of the United Nations when some world leaders stand to deliver their address, some delegates walk out but here respect for everyone is, and will remain, the key to ties of friendship and togetherness,"* he explains.

Supporting St.Ange's view of the carnival, Canadian journalist Carol Perhudof said that she has come to believe that the Carnaval International de Victoria could help to change the world because it's a celebration of every culture together. *"The Seychelles Carnival is a brilliant tourism idea that helps bring us to a point where we can live in harmony beyond colour of skin, to live in peace with each other,"* said Perehudoff, after her first visit for Seychelles Fourth International Carnival.

Through this 'Carnival of Carnivals', St.Ange has no doubt embarked on a global multicultural movement where people can capture the spirit of 'internationalism' to gain a better understanding and appreciation of another country's culture. Seychelles Carnival has captured the interest of leaders, tourism officials and travellers alike from the world over. As word spreads near and far among VIPs, media sources and curious tourists, the carnival has continued to get more popular each year. So just what is it about St.Ange that has allowed him to be able to successfully devise such an ingenious way to propel people and nations to come together under one accord?

For one thing, he has been dubbed a master marketer and promoter by International Kreole Magazine, published in the UK, as he was able to turn around visitation numbers to substantially increase tourism arrivals in Seychelles. Implementing and forging the tourism portfolio set forth by President James Michel, St.Ange's tourism approach and marketing methods have proven to be extremely effective, garnering him invitations from a host of countries and organizations that want to learn about the 'Seychelles Tourism Brand' as a guide for replication."

An article titled 'Destination Marketing: The Quest for Funds' by Anita Mendiratta, CNN Task Group / eTN sums it up; *"It is no surprise, therefore, that the Honourable Minister of Tourism and Culture of Seychelles, Alain Saint-Ange, takes his role as champion of the sector very seriously, doing all possible to stretch resources – time, money, people, intelligence – to the point of unprecedented return. For this reason, within the global tourism community, he, like his island nation, is viewed as somewhat of a natural phenomena.*❦

For more information visit www.seychelles.travel

Check List for Eco-Conference Venue Selection

Growing worldwide awareness of sustainability is placing pressure on the events organising industry to move in that direction, or it will surely lose business. Vague statements of being eco-friendly will not do and is simply seen as green washing, writes **Des Langkilde.**

Professional Conference Organisers (PCOs), Destination Management Companies (DMCs) and their clients need facts, figures or certification to prove unequivocally that the green credentials of a conference venue are above board. The Southern Africa Tourism Services Association (SATSA) held its 2014 conference at the Fair Trade certified Spier Wine Farm for this reason, and found the venue to comply with many of the check list items shown at the end of this article.

Benefits of Event Greening

Many international clients who bring their events to South Africa are making event greening a part of their tender requirements. According to Tourism Minister Derek Hanekom's opening address at Meetings Africa 2015, South Africa has already secured 177 major international association meetings for the next five years – thereby attracting a quarter of a million delegates with an estimated economic impact of R3,5 billion.

Greening your event should not only reduce the negative environmental impact, but should also leave a positive and lasting legacy for the local community. The following are some of the positive benefits for the organisers, participants, service providers and the local community that should be considered:

- **Cost savings:** Conserving energy, reducing waste, purchasing local products, and simply consuming less can save money.
- **Positive reputation:** A green event is a very visible demonstration of your client's commitment to sustainability, and your support of global actions against the negative influence of global warming. This also increases the marketing value of your organisation.
- **Environmental innovation:** Greening efforts promote innovative technologies and techniques, which help us to use resources more efficiently.
- **Raising awareness:** Each event offers a unique opportunity to raise awareness among participants, staff, service providers and the local community about the benefits of sustainable living, and enhances environmental best practice in the region.
- **Social benefits:** If planned and implemented carefully, the event could benefit the local region through creating jobs, selecting regional suppliers, promoting better working conditions and acting as a catalyst for social improvement.
- **Influencing decision-making:** By sharing standards, and introducing new ways of behaviour, other organisations could be motivated to introduce environmental and social improvements in their events as well.

- **Return on investment:** By pursuing greening, you will not only reduce costs, but also increase strategic opportunities.

Before you decide on the extent of greening your event, you need to consider the following:

- **How green do you want to go?** If it is the first time you are doing it, implement a few basic principles that are effective, and improve on these over time. Set goals so that you know what you are aiming for.
- **Does your team know what to do?** Take time to explain what you are doing, and why you are doing it, so that they can actively participate in the greening process. It should not be a once-off, but a mind shift.
- **Who are the key role players in the greening of your event?** Consider how you can bring your clients, sponsors and service providers on board to assist you with your greening efforts.
- **Who is your target audience?** What would their level of understanding and expectations be? International events will have to be more pro-active in implementing event-greening practices.
- **How do you inform delegates about the event greening?** You need to explain what you are doing, and encourage delegates to actively participate where possible. They can contribute to your greening efforts if you provide a multi-bin system for waste separation at source, or if you assist delegates to offset their carbon emissions for attending the event.
- **How will you measure your success?** If you cannot measure it, you cannot manage it. Get a few practical targets that you can aim for, and benchmark them against other events. Build on existing resources, and focus on activities that are achievable. Your goals need to be SMART (Specific, Measurable, Attainable, Realistic and Timely).

Yellow wood tree seedlings being propagated at Spier Wine Farm to offset the carbon footprint of conferences hosted at their venues.

Staff at the Spier Wine Farm waste separation and recycling plant.

Green Venue Check List

Accommodation establishments make heavy demands on natural resources (water and energy), and create large amounts of waste on a daily basis. With the proper policies and practices in place, it is possible to reduce these demands considerably. The National Minimum Standard for Responsible Tourism (SANS 1162:2011) was published by the SABS on 31 March 2011. This standard establishes specific minimum requirements for the performance of organisations in the tourism sector in relation to sustainability, and enables an organisation to formulate a policy and objectives, which take into account legal requirements and information pertaining to the impact of these requirements. When considering a venue or accommodation establishment, similar considerations need to be taken into account.

By way of example, I've used the Spier Wine Farm to tick-off against the following check list:

☑ **Environmental Policy.** Does the venue have one? This should ideally be displayed at their entrance, and should be easily accessible.

☑ **Environmental Management System** (EMS). Does the venue have any recognized environmental rating?

☑ **Eco-procurement policy.** Does this give preference to environmentally friendly and locally sourced goods and services?

☑ **Waste Management.** Check on status and availability as well as who manages this, or whether this has to be factored in as an extra cost for your event.

☑ **Recycling Programme.** Does the venue have one?
  • Check for major waste streams, such as glass, tin, plastic, paper

Spier Wine Farm's vlei and reed beds recycle 'grey' waste water for re-use in farm irrigation.

and organic waste. If they do, ask for more details about how this works, and who is responsible to ensure that the waste is recycled and not sent to a landfill site.
  • Check whether they (or their sub-contractor) will be able to provide waste separation at source, on-site or off-site, that will comply with the anticipated waste streams of your event.
  • Check whether they (or their sub-contractor) will be able to provide you with statistics on the type, volume and weight of the recycled waste and sent to a landfill site.
  • Encourage a multi-bin system at source to reduce contamination of waste. Note that venues often have a system in place for their own affairs, but not for events hosted at their venue.

☑ **Air Conditioning.** Can the venue give you the option of using natural ventilation? Not only is this is energy efficient, but usually also pleasant for the delegates as opposed to sitting in a cold, stuffy venue. If possible, the use of air conditioning should be kept to a minimum, and should be set according to seasonal demand.

☑ **Lighting.** Do the main access areas have energy-efficient lighting, such as CFLs (compact fluorescent lights) or LEDs (light-emitting diodes)? Ask whether it is possible to dim lights (50%) during build-up and breakdown days, and still comply with safety regulations.

☑ **Energy.** Can the venue provide you with energy from renewable energy sources, such as solar, wind or RECs?

☑ **Water Efficiency.** Are all toilets and taps water efficient? e.g. are toilets fitted with a dual-flush device, interruptible flush system, small cistern or displacement device, or set optimally in the case of flushmaster systems.

☑ **Environmental Training.** Do staff members receive environmental training? If so, enquire about details to determine the level of understanding and support that you could expect from staff members around greening issues.

☑ **Transport.** Is the venue within safe walking or cycling distance to accommodation, shops, entertainment areas, etc? If so, this will contribute to reducing the carbon footprint impact on your eco-conference. At the very least, is the venue close to public transport connections?

☑ **Corporate Social Investment** (CSI). Does the venue have a CSI programme in place? If so, ask for details to see how they support their local community, and promote local economic ▶

A candle lit buffet at Spier Wine Farm's Manor House Courtyard provides an ideal solution to eco-conference energy saving objectives.

development. You might even be able to contribute to their CSI programme through your event.

✔ **Chemicals.** Does the venue use biodegradable and/or non-toxic cleaning chemicals?

✔ **Water.** Can the venue provide refillable jugs of water instead of plastic bottles of water for delegates? Also check whether they can provide glasses instead of disposable cups at water coolers in the venue.

✔ **Food and Beverages.** Can the venue provide Green choices? These choices may include:

- **Local, seasonal and organic:** Menus that reflect locally sourced seasonal produce. Out-of-season items are usually grown in hot houses, or have to be flown in – both resulting in high carbon emissions. Organic food is a good choice, because it is grown without any pesticides, artificial fertilisers or genetic modification.
- **Responsible green suppliers**: If using an outside caterer, set a specific percentage of items that have to be local, fair-trade or organic.
- **Fair trade:** International rating systems provide credibility, and ensure that the benefits (premium paid on the product) actually reach the beneficiaries.
- **Food miles:** Refers to the distance that food has travelled from field to plate – it is best to eat food with low food miles, because it would be fresher, and would have a smaller carbon footprint.
- **Less meat:** Offer vegetarian meal options, and where possible, minimise the quantity of red meat offered. Meat production accounts for considerably more carbon emissions compared to non-meat products.
- **Healthy choices:** Provide healthier options, such as seasonal fruit platters, at teatime, and ensure that other main meals automatically include low-GI (glycaemic index) and low-fat food choices. These have the added benefit of regulating delegates' energy and concentration levels.
- **Marine conservation:** If fish or seafood in on the menu, ensure that these are sourced from sustainable marine resources. Check the fish species status at *www.wwfsassi.co.za* for endangered species information.
- **Leftover food:** Try to establish the exact number of delegates

to avoid wastage. Arrange with a local charity organisation to collect leftover food, such as FoodBank *www.foodbank.org.za*
- **Cutlery and crockery:** Avoid the use of disposable items, as these mostly end up on a landfill site.
- **Buy bulk, and re-use:** Provide beverages in bulk, i.e. fruit juice and fresh water on tables, instead of separate juice boxes and water bottles. Avoid single-use containers, such as sugar sachets, but rather provide a sugar dispenser. Avoid unnecessary disposable items, such as plastic straws and plastic coffee stirrers. **it**

More resources on the subject of Eco-Confererncing can be found at:

Spier Wine Farm: *www.spier.co.za*
Event Greening Forum: *www.eventgreening.co.za*
Fair-trade: *www.fairtrade.org.za*
Fair Trade in Tourism South Africa: *www.fairtourismsa.org.za*
Forest Stewardship Council: *www.fsc.org*
Green Building Council of South Africa: *www.gbcsa.org.za*
GreenStaySA: *www.greenstaysa.org.za*
Greenstuff: *www.greenstuff.co.za*
Heritage SA: *www.heritageza.co.za*
Organics: *www.bdoca.co.za*
South African Bureau of Standards: *www.sabs.co.za*
Southern African Sustainable Seafood Initiative: *www.wwfsassi.co.za*
Energy Star: *www.energystar.gov*

The laundry service at Spier Wine Farm uses only biodegradable detergents.

Thrivability in Green Hotel Development

A recently launched hotel management company plans to expand its 'Greenest Hotel' concept across Africa, and backs-up its claim with some convincing facts and figures, writes **Des Langkilde.**

I've always known the verb 'thrive' as meaning to prosper or flourish, but the word 'thrivability' is new to me.

I recently heard the term while attending a presentation at WTM-Africa in Cape Town, presented by Samantha Annandale, General Manager of Hotel Verde. In her presentation, she defined 'thrivability' as "Hospitality solutions that are not only sustainable but Thrivable: incorporating people, profit and planet. The language of sustainability is about neutralising. Thrivability is about succeeding."

Whether or not thrivability is just a word game or something larger and more inclusive than sustainability – it is a stronger term for what hospitality businesses (should) aim for. Thrivability speaks to the business imperative of making profit in order to perpetuate an organization (and its members/employees) as well as function in productive symbiosis with its environment.

Announcing Verde Hotels expansion plans into Africa, Samantha Annandale shared some interesting facts – an unusual act of transparency not often divulged by hoteliers.

In comparing and quantifying the Return On Investment (ROI) between building a green hotel versus a traditional hotel, she said that Hotel Verde's flagship project located in Cape Town International Airport's industrial zone, cost R187 million to build, which included the premium for building green, compared to R1.15 million per key without the green technology premium. An average traditional hotel will cost on average between R1.3 to R1.5 million per key without the green technology.

Isolating quantifiable ROI's, the green build project gained just over R30 million in free press exposure since the project commenced, reduced utility consumption costs by 70% (cost per room night based on utilities at Hotel Verde is R29.52 vs an average Cape Town hotel of R97.28 cost), and lowered energy consumption by 70,79% (77 kWh/sqm/annum vs Cape Town hotel average of 255 kWh/sqm/annum), which even beat the LEED model average of 144 kWh/sqm/annum by 46,53%.

Overall, the Hotel Verde green-build project resulted in 35% lower operating costs, a 70% reduction in energy consumption, 85% waste to landfill reduction, and 35% lower water consumption.

"It is the strong belief of the Verde Hotels team and myself that the hotel industry has changed, and that we simply cannot build or operate hotels in the same way that we have done for the past twenty years. Verde Hotels is the future of hospitality. Companies with proactive environmental strategies have a 4% higher return on investment, 9% higher sales growth and 17% higher operating growth than companies with poor environmental track records," said Samantha Annandale in conclusion of her presentation.

As if echoing her sentiments, Hotel Verde was awarded the global Green Hotelier of 2015, Africa and the Middle East award. This award adds to the hotel's already impressive array of accolades.

As a hotel management company, Verde Hotels aims to spearhead sustainable hotel management throughout Africa by offering hotel investors and developers property management packages for both new construction projects and retrofitting of existing buildings. it

For more information visit www.verdehotels.co.za or www.hotelverde.co.za or email bookings @hotelverde.co.za

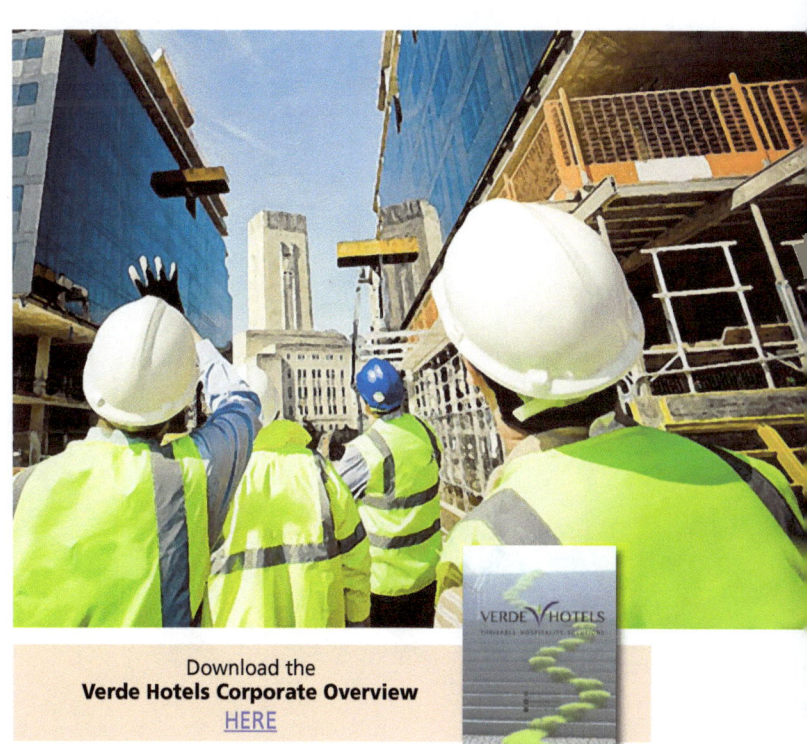

Download the
Verde Hotels Corporate Overview
HERE

Property Review
Hotel Verde
Cape Town, South Africa

Airport Industria is not an address which inspires images of 'environmentally-friendly' or 'carbon neutral', but Hotel Verde is both these things, writes **Kirsten Bohle**.

Universally Accessible. *Hotel Verde offers two rooms that accommodate and meet the international standards of universally accessible design.*

Nestled amongst the parking lots of rental car companies and industrial warehouses, a stone's throw from Cape Town International Airport, the self-proclaimed Greenest Hotel in Africa has gone above and beyond to ensure that their operation has no negative impact on their surrounding environment. More so, the wetlands which serve as the hotel gardens have been restored back to their former glory after years of environmental abuse from the surrounding industries.

Every aspect of the hotel which could be 'greened' has been, and helpful signs located all around the hotel and in the rooms explain how this has been achieved. A *Pontos* grey water plant sterilises and filters bath water, which is pumped back into the hotel to flush toilets. The hotel has a 40 000 litre water tank to collect rainwater, three wind turbines, which generate energy and photovoltaic panels for powering essential hardware. LED bulbs light the hotel and a vegetable garden is tended to by the kitchen staff. Any other food served in the dining room is sourced and produced locally. Their design piece **de resistance** is a living wall (or vertical garden) separating the lounge from the bar, which is not only a calming beauty but also helps to purify the air inside.

Environmental Design Award

Tourism Tattler was invited for an over-night stay to celebrate the Hotel's latest and greatest achievement – a Leadership in Energy and Environmental Design (LEED) Platinum Certificate for new construction – the only hotel in Africa to have qualified for this honour and one of only six worldwide. The program recognizes the best-in-class green building practices, with platinum being the highest level to reach. Hotel Verde's status as Africa's Greenest Hotel has been firmly cemented.

Every Wednesday evening, the hotel observes earth hour. The lights are switched off and dinner is served in candlelight, to the sweet tunes of the resident pianist. The kitchen cooks with as little electricity as possible on a Wednesday and we were treated to a *potjie* buffet and gentle crème brulee for dessert. Just after nine the house lights came on, assaulting our eyes and after a quick poll the diners unanimously agreed to continue our meals in the glow of candlelight.

The owners of the hotel, Mario and Annemarie Delicio, conceptualised the hotel from the ground up with the help of several dedicated experts, including sustainability consultant Andre Harms of Ecolution Consulting. He credits his clients for their dedication to the concept, which did not come cheap or easy.

They were inspired to create an entirely carbon-neutral hotel and conferencing experience, catering not only to business travel but also to holiday tourists looking for a convenient base close to both the airport and Cape Town's favourite attractions. It is their belief that all hotels should be built in this manner and should strive to be eco-friendly.

Outdoor gym. *Hotel Verde is the first hotel in Africa to showcase power generating gym equipment.*

Music corner. *Encourages guests to pick up an instrument and allow their creative juices to flow.*

Eco-pool. *Another first for Hotel Verde, the eco-pool is completely harmless to the environment using no harmful chemicals. It recreates the natural system of wetlands to clean itself offering a pool that is not only better for the environment but better for guests too.*

Superior Facilities and Amenities

Luxury, style and convenience have not been compromised in the quest for carbon-neutral. The artwork in the hotel is all locally sourced and the rooms boast a contemporary design with large showers and a bed you can't wait to sink into. The rooms come equipped with minibars, flat screen televisions and free Wi-Fi is available throughout the hotel. Guests are also invited to take a dip in the eco-pool or a turn around the jogging trail, which winds through the restored wetlands. An outdoor gym makes for a fun pit stop on your route, while the beehives might make you pick up your pace. A gym is also available inside, and your workout on the machines will generate power which is pumped back into the hotel. Guests are encouraged to utilise this service to earn *Verdinos*, which are rewarded for eco-friendly behaviour and can be redeemed at the twenty four hour deli in the reception area. Not using the air conditioner in your room is another way to earn Verdinos, as is recycling waste and reusing bath towels.

It is the little touches that set's a hotel apart in the eyes of a seasoned traveller, the details overlooked by many hotels and guesthouses. A unique music corner encourages guests to pick up an instrument and allow their creative juices to flow, which is just one way that Hotel Verde demonstrates their excellence in customer care. Serving breakfast from 4:30 a.m. is another, welcome news indeed for red-

eye travellers more accustomed to a breakfast of instant coffee and not much else.

Hotel Verde ticks all the boxes and then some. Comfort, style and guest satisfaction appear to be as high a priority to them as ensuring the environmental sustainability of running the 145 room hotel. With 7 conference venues accommodating 4-120 delegates, Hotel Verde will meet the most deserning PCO's conferencing needs and more.

The hotel is very conveniently located and offers a great variety of activities and facilities for their guests, all offered with a friendly smile. They are currently running several winter specials for both their conference and overnight facilities. If you are planning group tours to Cape Town, book your clients in now. Not only will your clients be pampered, they will also be able to brag that they have stayed at Africa's greenest hotel. **it**

About the Author: *Tourism Tattler correspondent* **Kirsten Bohle** *is a freelance writer and blogger, about to embark on a six month trip through South Asia. She holds a BA International Studies from Stellenbosch University, with majors in Political Science, History and Psychology. This was followed up by a Post Graduate Diploma in Marketing and Advertising Communications. She writes at* www.thejollyjammer.co.za.

Rooms. *All boast a contemporary design with large showers and a bed you can't wait to sink into.*

Jogging Trail. *The 320 metre long trail meanders through wetland, which flourishes with flora and birdlife.*

Fostering a Sustainable Hospitality Industry

In celebrating Earth Day 2015, a local green cleaning product manufacturer encouraged the hospitality industry to adopt sustainable practices to safeguard the environment, its guests and its employees, writes **Raynique Ducie.**

How many beds are there in the hospitality industry nationwide? If each bed in every room in all hotels, guest houses, lodges, long-stay apartments or bed and breakfasts is fitted with a sheet, a blanket, a comforter and at least two pillows – how much laundry does that equate to daily? How many bathrooms, kitchens and dining halls must be cleaned? How many dishes must be disinfected in the restaurant sector? Safety standards require that this industry focuses on sanitation, but this does not require the use of harsh chemicals that damage the environment.

On April 22nd the world celebrated Earth Day. According to the Earth Day Network, this year is the 45th anniversary of Earth Day and could be the most exciting year in environmental history: the year in which economic growth and sustainability join hands; the year in which world leaders finally pass a binding climate change treaty; the year in which citizens and organizations divest from fossil fuels and put their money into renewable energy solutions. These are tough issues but the future of our planet and the survival of life on earth are at stake. "On Earth Day we need you to take a stand so that together, we can show the world a new direction. It's our turn to lead. So our world leaders can follow by example." The aim is to redefine what progress looks like, with the motto "It's Our Turn to Lead".

In celebrating Earth Day, a local green cleaning product manufacturer encouraged the hospitality industry to adopt sustainable practices to safeguard the environment, its guests and its employees. "The extent of the damage that chemical products have on the environment, on the health of those that use it, and on the people that are exposed to it cannot be overstated," says Clinton Smith of Green Worx Cleaning Solutions.

Although a recent study indicated that consumers avoid utilising green cleaning products due to the perception that they are more costly than traditional products, the reality is that enzyme based products are more concentrated, are more efficient, and are therefore more cost effective. The enzymes digest host material where the germ and odour causing bacteria live and reproduce.

When ensuring that their facilities are sufficiently sanitised, accommodation providers should focus on utilising safe, non-toxic products that are effective and reliable. Where facility management services are utilised, industry leaders should exert pressure on these organisations to implement green practices.

"If each industry takes responsibility for the effects that its actions have on the environment, true change can be effected," concludes Smith. **it**

For more information visit **www.green-worxcs.co.za**

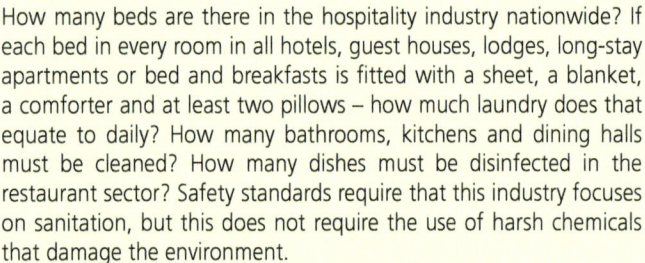

Reviving legends and all that jazz

The KwaZulu-Natal South Coast is well remembered by many through their childhood memories of warm sunshine, sandy feet, family hotels, the charm of seaside resorts and the sound of seagulls calling for their souci, writes **Nikki Tilley**.

The rooftop Skybar at DesRoches Hotel and Conference Centre in Margate.

Fast forward to 2015 where the old seaside legends such as the ever-popular Blue Marlin Hotel are being revived.

The Blue Marlin Hotel in Scottburgh on KwaZulu-Natal's (KZN) South Coast, was officially re-launched on Friday 10th April, following the completion of a R 35 million renovation programme, that began two years ago. The renovations have seen a total transformation of all rooms and outdoor areas, making this property the only resort of its kind on the KZN upper south coast.

This now provides a new good quality, affordable, relaxing destination for both South African and international tourists and business people, especially considering the wealth of excellent golf courses nearby and being right on the doorstep of one of the top ten dive sites in the world (with Protea Banks, also on the South Coast, mere 40 minute drive further down south).

And of course, the South Coast is not just about beaches. Take a drive into the hinterland and meet the Ingeli Forest Lodge, nestled below the Ingeli Mountain range near Kokstad, still one of the best kept secrets around. Built in the 1960's, it was a regular stop for travellers en-route between the Transkei and Durban. Extensive renovations began two years, which has resulted into what can only be described as a little piece of heaven.

It is surrounded by breathtaking indigenous forests, which has become home to many events including the breathtaking Ingeli Skyrun, held in April each year, attracting participants from all over South Africa. Here you can experience some of the very best outdoor activities including the best mountain biking and trail running routes, as well as great hiking/walking, birding and exploring opportunities. You will be spoilt for choice with forest, natural bush and mountains right on your doorstep. Also geared for younger kids, Ingeli have gone out of their way paying attention to every detail and putting on a brand new 18-hole Adventure Golf course, jungle gym and play area, supervised Playroom and Pump Track.

And just few months back, Margate saw four star DesRoches Hotel and Conference Centre being opened. Previously a 'fun world' with ten pin bowling, this magnificent new addition to the skyline is something to see for yourself. The owners have stopped at nothing. With everything that shuts and closes, private dining rooms, the glorious rooftop Skybar, spas and kid friendly areas – who would have thought this possible only a few years ago?

So why all this investment into property on the south coast? Because clearly it's worth it. And facts and figures are starting to show just that.

I guess it's time then to revisit a legend and discover the new.

For more information visit www.tourismsouthcoast.co.za it

Franchising: Preferred for Hotel Expansion

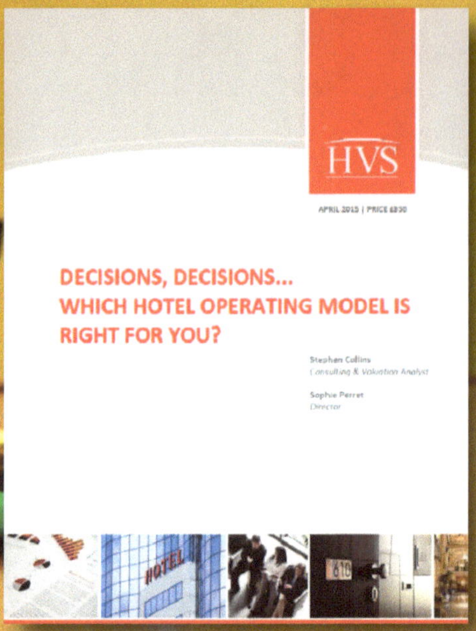

Over half of the world's hotels are now branded properties, with franchising being the operating model of choice for most of the large hotel operators, according to a new report from hotel consultancy HVS London, writes **Linda Pettit**.

**DECISIONS, DECISIONS...
WHICH HOTEL OPERATING MODEL IS
RIGHT FOR YOU?**

Stephen Collins
Consulting & Valuation Analyst

Sophie Perret
Director

Five of the largest branded hotel companies (IHG, Accor, Marriott, Hilton and Starwood) make up 30% of the current global branded room supply and 65% of the development pipeline, which demonstrates the increasing shift away from independently operated hotels worldwide.

The report, which examines trends in the way hotels are being operated, identifies the proliferation in the number of players and stakeholders that can be involved in a successful hotel – including brand owners, owners and management companies as well as a combination of operating models and hybrid models.

There is also a geographical difference. Across Europe, where independent hotels are more common, franchises account for 50% of rooms in the large listed hotel companies sampled by HVS, with the owned and leased model making up approximately 30% of room counts, and management contracts around 20%.

This contrasts sharply with the North American market, where 85% of the research sample were franchised, just 13% under management contracts and only 2% were owned and leased properties.

NORTH AMERCIA VS EUROPEAN OPERATING MODELS IN MAJOR HOTEL CHAINS

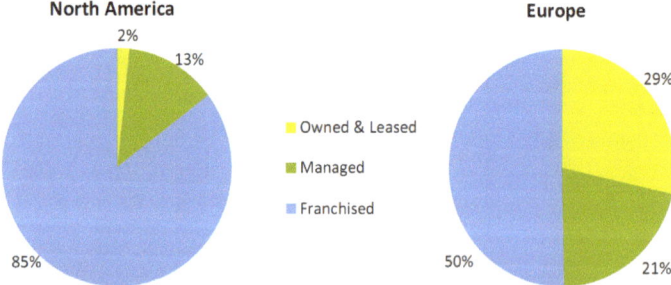

Companies sampled include Accor, IHG, Hilton, Hyatt and Marriott. Source: HVS research

Says report co-author Stephen Collins, consulting & valuation analyst with HVS London: *"In the US the franchise sector is highly regulated, making it more transparent and easier to compare the results of one brand against another. In Europe franchise regulations differ from one country to another, making it more difficult to compare like-for-like."*

HVS also identifies the growing use of Third Party Operators (TPOs) to operate franchises, bridging the gap between the owner of the hotel and the franchisors who own the brand.

"While many franchisees are owner-operators and have the management expertise to be successful, there remains a gap between owners that are unable or unwilling to control the daily operations of the hotel and the franchisors that provide the brand," said HVS director Sophie Perret.

"This is where third-party operators have come into prominence. TPOs have allowed companies to sell their flag first and direct their management efforts towards the hotels and brands they deem appropriate, while the owner is able to realise advantages of both franchises and management agreements while avoiding a number of the limitations.

"The franchise model, with or without a third party operator, is expected to carry on gaining momentum in Europe, as it continues to deliver better value for all parties involved," she added.

The report concludes that in the coming years, franchising will likely continue to gain ground as the preferred operating model for a number of reasons: major chains have placed increasing emphasis on franchising to meet their desired expansion page; TPOs have proven competent in bridging the gap between owners and brand companies; and small independent hotels in secondary locations turn to flexible, less-standardised franchisors to remain competitive.

With that said, there will never be a one-size-fits-all operating model, The experience and risk appetite of the owner, the size and standard of the property, and the suitability and availability of potential brands are but a few of the components that factor into which model is most suitable.

To download the report, **Decisions, Decisions: Which hotel operating model is right for you?** *by Stephen Collins and Sophie Perret, click* here.

About HVS: HVS is the world's leading consulting and services organization focused on the hotel, mixed-use, shared ownership, gaming, and leisure industries. For more information visit www.hvs.com

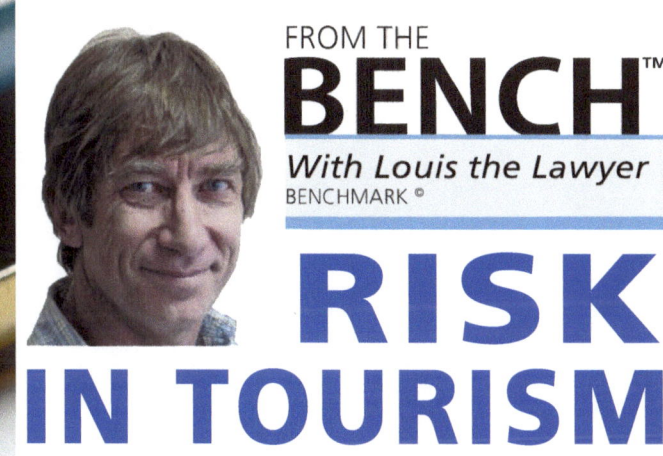

Legal

FROM THE BENCH™

With Louis the Lawyer
BENCHMARK ©

RISK IN TOURISM

– PART 10 –
THE LAW: CONTRACTS

In **Part 1** (*page 36* <u>August 2014</u>), I categorised risk into five categories, namely; **1. PEOPLE, 2. MONEY, 3. LAW, 4. SERVICE** and **5. ECOLOGY.** I will be dealing with the risk profile of each, i.e. broadly speaking the areas of risk that any business is exposed to can been allocated under these five categories.

In **Part 2**, (*page 22* <u>September 2014</u>), I covered the category of **'People'** under four sub-categories: **Staff** (discussed in Part 1); **Third party service providers ('TPSP')**; and **Business Associates**.

Part 3 (*page 24* <u>October 2014</u>), continued with 'PEOPLE' as **Customers**.

Part 4 (*page 27* <u>November 2014</u>), started the discussion on the 2nd category, namely **'MONEY'** in terms of CASH and CHEQUES.

Part 5 (*page 23* <u>December 2014</u>), looked at CREDIT and CREDIT CARDS.

Part 6 (*page 25* <u>January 2015</u>), looked at **LAW** and CONTRACTS, with an introduction and Requisite #1: Offer & Acceptance.

Part 7 (*page 18* <u>February 2015</u>), continued with Requisite #1 covering telephone enquiries, e-mails, websites and advertising.

Part 8 (*page 17* <u>March 2015</u>), covered Requisites #2: Legally Binding Obligation, and #3: Consensus in contracts.

Part 9 (*page 20* <u>April 2015</u>), covered Requisite #4: Perfromance Must Be Possible.

REQUISITE #5: PERFORMANCE MUST BE PERMISSIBLE

The performance envisaged by the parties and provided for in the agreement must be permissible in terms of the current legal regime. The legal regime entails not only the laws that appear on the statute books, but also the custom and norms of society.

All businesses are waging an ongoing battle with the collection of monies due to them and bad debts. They stick to the letter of the law, but get nowhere: summonses cannot be served; judgments cannot be executed, etc. As a result debt collectors (the baseball bat and hard hat brigade) has been resorted to by many a legitimate business.

The contractual terms of these 'gentlemen' may vary from simply requiring the debt collector to collect the amount outstanding for a fee to a requirement that 50% of the debt be paid up front as a deposit. If the creditor wishes to enforce any term of this contract e.g. to have his deposit returned because the debt has not been collected, he will not be able to do so. This is because contracts of this nature is *contra bonos mores* (against the goods norms and morals of society). You are not allowed to take the law into your own hands. Accordingly the contract will be null and void and no rights or liabilities will flow from it, and if you have paid a deposit, you will have to forfeit it as you have no enforceable contract/ right to enforce! I have over the years had to assist two aggrieved parties with such contracts and unfortunately had to be the bearer of bad tidings!

Likewise a bribery agreement is void per se (Extel Industrial vs Crown Mills 1999 SCA) and therefore unenforceable. An agreement designed to mislead creditors (e.g. a marriage of convenience in this case) is immoral and against public policy and thus *void ab initio* (Maseko vs Maseko 1992 W).

REQUISITE #6: CAPACITY OF THE CONTRACTING PARTIES

Something that is often glossed over is whether or not the person you are dealing with has the capacity to contract or has been duly authorized by the party or parties he or she purports to represent. What we are alluding to are such matters as the age of the party, transactions on behalf companies or group bookings.

As the law stands at the moment following recent legislation, the age at which any individual can enter into a binding contract is 18. Any agreement with a party under that age will NOT constitute a binding and legally enforceable contract unless such a party is emancipated (see below) or the parent or guardian has signed the agreement. OK, you may be thinking, this kind of thing simply does not happen. Let me tell you, you may as well bet your bottom dollar because it does. I recently had the case of a youth booking with a Johannesburg based travel agent and travelling all over Europe. When the youth returned the travel agent approached her for payment of the balance of the trip, but no payment was forthcoming. Many telephone calls later they approached the parents who (No doubt after speaking with a friend in the legal fraternity) declined to pay, insisting that they knew nothing about it and that the travel agents sole right of recourse was against the child, which was of course based on a contract that was null and void!

A more prevalent situation which has criminal sanctions, is the employment of an under age (18) person. Again such a contract will not be enforceable. There is the issue of emancipation which means that a person under the age of 18 may be deemed to have reached maturity due to certain business dealings or via a court order, but it would be better not to attempt going down that road – it is simply too complex.

It is therefore imperative when you enter into ANY contract with ANY individual that you obtain a copy of their identity document. It is not only good risk management but also good business practice. It will provide you with irrefutable proof of the persons age and if under 18, you will have to obtain the signature of a parent or legal guardian of the person. Do NOT enter into any transaction without doing that, e.g. make reservations with airlines, hotels etc. as you will have NO right of recourse and will have to put your hand into your OWN pocket!! It will also be a great help if the person were to become a debtor/does not pay and vanishes – an ID number is crucial in order to trace a person. it

4 Myths Related to Guest Feedback

Here are four common myths that hoteliers believe about guest feedback and online reputation management, and the truth associated with those myths, writes **RJ Friedlander**.

TripAdvisor's recent TripBarometer Report showed that 60% of hoteliers surveyed were planning on investing more in online reputation management (ORM) in 2015. If you are planning on investing in ORM this year, it is important that you have a proper understanding of the concept of Guest Intelligence, prior to doing so. Guest Intelligence is the in-depth analysis of online reviews and guest satisfaction survey data – which includes both during, and post-stay surveys, to provide detailed insight into what guests like and dislike about their stay, and determine how to improve your property's service.

Here's my top four myths related to managing online and direct guest feedback, along with the best practices that will help you to improve your property's Guest Intelligence results.

Myth 1: Online reputation management (ORM) & guest surveys are two separate data sets.

Truth: Many hotels collect and use ORM and guest survey data separately and some even have different departments handling the two types of data. In spite of this, analytics of the two are much more actionable and effective when used together. Only by collecting and examining both online review data and direct guest survey data, will you be able to get a detailed and accurate picture of your property's strengths and weaknesses, which will help you to prioritize internal action to improve guest satisfaction.

Myth 2: It is very difficult to improve your ranking on TripAdvisor and other key review sites.

Truth: This myth combines both fact and fiction. It is true that many hotels struggle to positively impact their overall rating and rankings on key review sites; however, this does not mean it is impossible. The key is to have enough detail in the information about what guests like and dislike about their stay. It stands to reason that if you don't understand how your guests are feeling, it will be very difficult to make the changes necessary to be able to improve guest satisfaction – and, as a result, your ranking on TripAdvisor, as well as other review sites.

However, if your brand and individual properties are equipped with the right Guest Intelligence solutions to properly understand the nuances of your guests' feedback, it becomes much easier to significantly increase your overall ratings and rankings. The final step is proactively encouraging your guests to write reviews about their experience. One program that many hoteliers have found to be very effective is the TripAdvisor's Review Collection Program, which incorporates the TripAdvisor questionnaire within the hotel's post-stay survey and, in most cases, creates a sizable increase in review volume.

Myth 3: More questions, the better.

Truth: It is a common misconception that the more questions you have on your guest survey, the more useful the information that it yields will be. In fact, at a certain point, the opposite is true for two important reasons: firstly, guests are often intimidated by lengthy, overly detailed surveys, especially when it asks questions that don't pertain to their stay, and will choose not to respond to the survey altogether; and secondly, because the most complete insight is obtained by asking the right questions to the right guest (a.k.a. quality over quantity).

Myth 4: If you only track what is being said about your property on the top international channels, it will be sufficient.

Truth: If you're not tracking responses and generating reviews in all of the relevant and influential OTAs and review sites for the segments of travellers that you're trying to reach, you are not likely to be optimizing your online distribution strategy. There are more than 142 online review sites that generate reviews in more than 45 original languages. The overall review score, department scores and sentiment of reviews posted about your property on each site can vary drastically depending on the cultural and demographic focus of a particular website.

As well, you limit your ability to drive bookings if you don't put a priority on the second-tier channels in the key markets where your clients originate. To address this issue, review your property's overall distribution strategy and ensure that you have a strong presence and positive reputation on all relevant regional and local channels.

To successfully increase guest satisfaction and to improve ADR and RevPAR, it is crucial that your property integrate Guest Intelligence into your operational plans for 2015 and beyond. **it**

*About the author: **RJ Friedlander** is the CEO of **ReviewPro** – a leading provider of Guest Intelligence solutions to independent hotel brands worldwide. The company's suite of cloud-based solutions includes Online Reputation Management (ORM) and Guest Survey Solution (GSS), which enable hoteliers to obtain deeper insight into operational and service strengths and weaknesses, increasing guest satisfaction, review volume and driving revenue. Visit www.reviewpro.com.*

Pros & Cons of Booking Restrictions

In this article **Jean Francois Mourier** outlines the most common hotel booking restrictions and when they are and aren't useful for increasing bookings and revenue.

Every hotelier has used a restriction in their pricing strategy at one time or another. Whether a minimum length of stay (MinLOS) requirement over a particularly busy period, or a restriction on a particular day preventing new arrivals (Closed to Arrival – CTA), these restrictions are a common business practice. But are they the best way to manage pricing and occupancy for a hotel on a day-to-day basis? In this article, I will cover the most commonly used restrictions and explain which one is the most important restriction that hoteliers should be using in today's highly competitive online marketing.

Minimum Length of Stay (MinLOS) Restriction

MinLOS restrictions were highly useful in the days prior to development and rise in popularity of the online booking channel, but today, where a large percentage of bookings are made online, they are not useful for day-to-day usage. However, MinLOS restrictions can be useful for special events or big-ticket days (like New Years Eve). Here's why this restriction is not useful day-to-day:

First and foremost, it restricts your potential guests' ability to book their stay according to their needs, not corporate policy. It is an inconvenience that will most likely send the potential guest running to the competition.

Secondly, you're decreasing your online visibility. By having a MinLOS restriction in place, any searches that customers make on the OTAs will filter out your property if the guests' stay isn't compatible. This decreases the billboard effect and can cost you valuable direct bookings in the long run.

To find out more about why hoteliers shouldn't use MinLOS, read 'The MLOS Myth'.

Closed to Arrival/Departure Restriction

If a hotelier decides to make a particular day "closed to arrival" or "closed to departure, it means that guests are restricted from either arriving or departing on that particular day. If a guest is already staying with the property on that date, they can continue their stay uninterrupted but no arrivals/departures will be allowed on that date.

These restrictions are most commonly used to control the flow of arrivals and departures, during special events when a certain stay pattern is desired, such as stays on the four days leading up to Super Bowl. However, I have seen an overuse of these restrictions to address short staffing and to facilitate the check-in and check-out process.

Once again, why would you make it more difficult for a guest to book with your property? If a guest wants to arrive or check-out on a given date, let them do so. If resources are an issue, consider alternatives like offering check-out via iPads in the lobby and getting a sophisticated PMS to make your reservation and check-in procedures less complicated.

Maximum Stay Restriction

This restriction does not allow guests to make bookings that extend beyond a certain number of days, and is often used when offering promotional discounts to drive occupancy such as 'Stay Three Nights, Get the Fourth Night Free'. I have seen cases where the hoteliers set a Maximum Stay restriction to avoid giving away two free nights if a guest wants to stay eight consecutive nights.

It seems pretty obvious to me that this restriction be counter-intuitive! A hotel's end goal is to increase bookings, which is why they offer a discount in the first place, but then, they tell their guest that they can't stay beyond a certain period of time. Promotional discounts seek to increase the volume of bookings. If you are penalizing your guests or not letting them book longer stays, you are closing the door and minimizing the amount that can be earned on incidentals during their stay, which is often how hoteliers increase their RevPAR on discounted promotional stays.

Finally, the holy grail of restrictions: Price.

Out of all of the restrictions that I outlined above, price is the only one that I would suggest that hoteliers use on a continuous basis. Other than price, overusing all of these restrictions is not beneficial because they all diminish the amount of revenue that a property can earn. That's where price is different.

Hoteliers should be aiming to sell the most rooms at the best rate, and competing on price makes that possible. The law of supply and demand tells us that to constrain demand, we can increase price (not exorbitantly unless you really want to limit sales). Similarly, to stimulate demand we can decrease price (incrementally – no rash discounting).

Do you still use these ineffective restrictions at your property? If so, try implementing price as your only restriction and watch your revenue grow! **it**

*About the author: Jean Francois Mourier is the CEO of **REVPAR GURU**, a company that provides hotels around the world with an alternative revenue management software solution, designed to deliver maximum bookings and profits. Visit www.revparguru.com*

Must Have Apps When Travelling

Business can increase with feature-rich applications that drive interest and engagement, writes **Grant Theis**.

Today we live in an era of engagement and as customers look to immerse themselves in brands and businesses, feature rich applications that provide content and engagement on the go and in the form that consumers want, have never been as important as they are today. And this is especially true for the retail and tourism industries.

MyGambia Travel App

The Official Gambia Travel Guide App offers a lot more than sun, sea and sand. With a population of under 2 million, Gambia is known for its diverse ecosystems around the central Gambia River. Abundant wildlife in its Kiang West National Park and Bao Bolong Wetland Reserve includes monkeys, hippos and rare birds.

The app is available on iTunes (compatible with iPhone, iPad, and iPod touch - iOS 7.0 or later) and for Android devices via GooglePlay.

In fact, applications have become as pervasive as the connectivity on which they depend and while they have become disruptive in the consumer space, as connectivity and capacity increases, the realisation that the enterprise space – such as retailers, hospitality and even big attraction venues - could use such applications to offer additional value add to both their process and their customers, is quickly coming to the fore. Consider such applications being used in core functions such as HR for increased workforce management, finance for streamlined billing services, operations or customer contact areas for increased collaboration and even areas such as marketing for enhanced customer relations.

Through advanced image recognition, augmented reality and proximity marketing through iBeacons – brands and places can come alive. What's more, merchants, hospitality chains and retailers are able to run unified marketing programs across multiple franchise locations, and, for the first time, unlock real-time attribution data, while simultaneously being able to self provide in-store vouchers, offers and loyalty programmes through such platforms – which means they are not only able to attract customers and tourists, but engage with them as well.

Today it is essential that consumers can engage with a business or brand on all mobile devices – and applications are the perfect platform to do so. What's more, once the business is out 'advertising' itself on such platforms, it also has a positive response from consumers who can now find information about places around them including the likes of restaurants, pubs, shopping, petrol stations, car rental, dentist, etc. By using location- based technology, the contact details for these places and built in maps to provide directions. When travelling, this is especially useful!

Technology is being used across the tourism industry to attract and engage with customers. And customers are demanding relevant information and ease of access to these businesses. When the two come together in a convenient feature-rich platform – they create a viable business eco-system.

About the author: Grant Theis is a co-founder of ttrumpet - an app for free calls and messaging worldwide, for vouchers, information, reviews, pricing and augmented reality. For more information visit www.ttrumpet.com

14 routes
6 cities
a whole lot of flying

When your customers want to go places,
kulula is the airline to take them there.

⊕ O.R. Tambo | ⊕ Lanseria | ⊕ Durbs | ⊕ Cape Town | ⊕ George | ⊕ East London

kulula.com

KINGJAMES 30444